Dedication

I hope the poems I have written replicate the idea of the movie "Certified Copy" by director Abbas Kiarostami. His poems were the ones that kickstarted my journey into writing poetry. Additionally, the ideas and inspiration of director Pa. Ranjith about the art of poetry initiated the expression of my emotions through my words.

Every step I take towards humanity feels like I am working for your dream, to Dr. B. R. Ambedkar and those who work for humanity.

Finally, I dedicate this book to one and all present here in this world.

Acknowledgements

I would like to thank every living and non-living organism in this world, with a special mention for ChatGPT.

Preface

I wrote this book to once again convey the fact: "No one can express your emotions better than you."

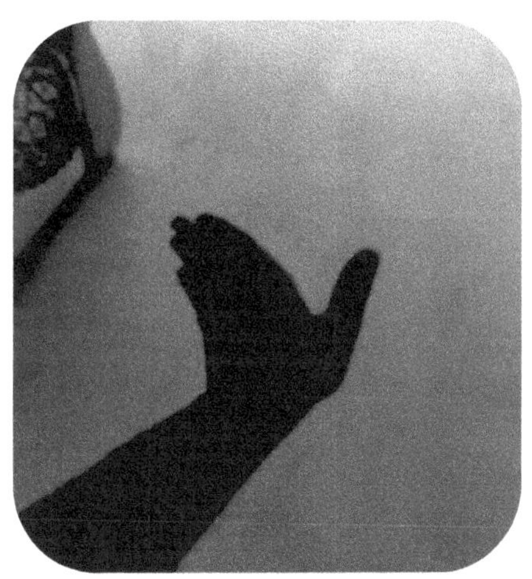

Welcome to a Life

❖ : Am I doing the right thing?
  : Maybe, But what is the right thing?

❖ : I would love to get lost in movies
  : I haven't played any character with you all,
    the moments we had are real
  : Or did I played another character!?

❖ When you need help, Look around you
  if no one is there, look inside you
  Life is precious, please save it

❖ Every character arc is Unfinished

❖ We love being ourselves,
  Yet, we love the shaped Garden

❖ It makes me happy,
that I can still watch people
from far like movies!

❖ Happy Teachers' Day
வாழ்வின் அனைத்துமே!

❖ When you have the clouds above you
which don't fall on you,
When you have the sun and moon with you
which don't make you slip,
When you have the tress around you
which don't cause you Dyspnea,

❖ பெண்ணொருத்தி கண்டேன்
பிறந்தநாள் விழாவினில்
புகுந்தவீட்டினை பிரியமுடியாமலும்
பிறந்தவீட்டினை அணைக்கமுடியாமலும்
நடுவில் நின்று
கண்ணீர் வடித்துக்கொண்டிருந்தாள்

❖ I walked a lot
  I explored a quite
  I enjoyed the view
  Routes were long
  Talks were endless
  I did what I planned
  And the day ended with a usual Sunset
  But something changed!

❖ The beauty of life
  is not in understanding!

❖ There are no copies

❖ I'm stuck, at that day
  When the trains were slow
  The air was new
  The day was calm

❖ Therla,
  Apdey pothu,

❖ It's so poetic
   The joy we had
   Thanks for your efforts
   in making me a human
   HANA

❖ We met them,
   in the conscious travel
   Shared snacks more than words
   We were old,
   They were young
   I forgot about the goodbye

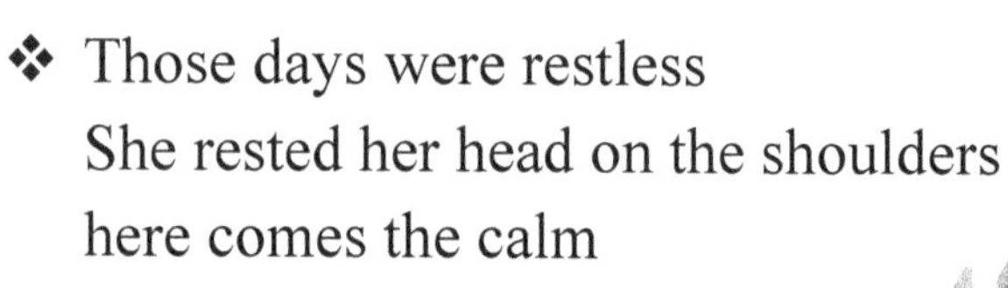

❖ Those days were restless
   She rested her head on the shoulders
   here comes the calm

❖   .,

❖ A forced poem:
That day I just went
inside the movie
"Taste of cherry"

❖ A forced poem:
Maybe I could've ended myself
Maybe I could've ended them
Maybe I could've ended it
Life goes on

❖ How I may felt
if I pushed you!?
I may have felt satisfied!
I may have jumped!
I may have cried!
I may have got beaten!
I may have missed hearing songs!
But thanks to me
I haven't done that

❖ Just another day
Looking at the sky through window
Invertedly

❖ That day,
  I think, I did like you said
  And I felt happiness

❖ Even though I missed you,
  I haven't tried to contact you
  But I had a belief
  "If you need something, you will get it"
  Thanks for breaking my stereotype
  It's your efforts which made me happy

❖ All my life I've seen you
  Here and there
  Sorry, I haven't observed you
  Hope, I will next time

❖ Even though it hurts
  It's happy to live in 'drama' genre

❖ The feelings I had
The house you had
The past I had
But the decision was made by me
To be happy

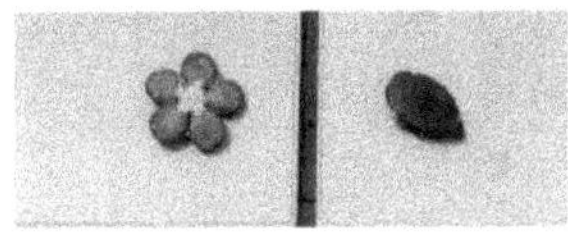

❖ Love
Love
Love
It is love
It's not love
It is love
It's not love
Life in the cycle of…

❖ I broke the walkman
which my brother gave me,
To make fan out of it,
But I ended up with DC motor

- ❖ A blurry connect
  Below the line
  An usual attraction
  (Un)expected connection
  Sync started perfection
  Selfless affection
  Open discussion
  A poignant friend

- ❖ It's a bokeh
  We can add any colour flower
  Whatever it is
  It's just a beauty

- ❖ Thanks for the bouquet
  It gives the opportunity to rearrange
  And add something new

- ❖ It's a bouquet
  We can add any colour flower
  Whatever it is
  It's just a beauty

❖ தேவையெற்ற நேரத்தில்
பொழியும் உன்மேல்
வன்மத்தை உமிழ்கிறேன்
இதுவரை உன்னை ரசித்ததாய்
ஞாபகமில்லை!
தேவையான நேரத்தில்
பொழியும் உன்னை
கொண்டாடும் எனக்கு
ஏனோ நெகிழியுனுள் வாழும் மக்களை
என் மணம் சிந்திக்கவில்லை!

❖ Art can't be copied

❖ The Eagerness, Hope, Anger
is not enough
to make the expectations of love
to go low

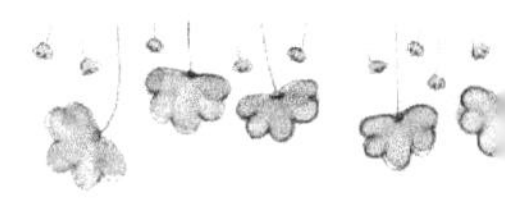

❖ I am happy that I have loved you
I am happy that I have let you go

❖ Motivation should be something
which explains the reality of illusion

❖ Yeah, of course,
Unexpected one gives bliss
but the expected one
Hits different

❖ Pain won't be a pain
once you understand
what that pain actually is

❖ Again!
On the crossroads
don't know
which one it's gonna be
or the still

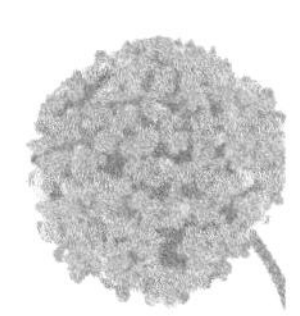

Hope the love returns

❖ Ney,
Even though I get ready
I stop myself
This is how it is

❖ Don't worry
I'll surprise you now and then
by
over-talking,
reflecting movies,
blocking you,
throwing away,
intro into unknown phase,
discussing,
abracadabra

❖ The life started to play in slow-mo
When I realized
Just being there
is more than anything;
Thank you to those
Who shared the earphones
and sorry to those
whose part I skipped

❖ : You just pulled me out of me
    and then
  : And then!?
  : And then…
    I don't know what's gonna happen!

❖ She ain't Miss World
   at least for others

❖ The more I love
   The far my mind likes to go
   looks like
   I am stuck in moral conflict

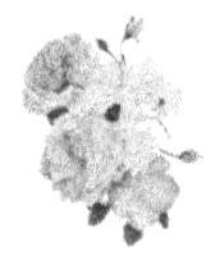

❖ The problem with surprise is
   It sometimes
   disappoints the unexpected ones
   Or may throw us into blurry

❖ When will we start working on
   Solutions,
   Before jumping into
   Prevention?

❖ நீ செய்யும் தவறையோ
   நீ ஏற்படுத்தும் வலியையோ
   சுட்டிக்காட்டுபவர்களை
   எதிரில் வைத்து பார்க்கவேண்டிய
   அவசியமில்லை

❖ I feel the insecurity when someone
   insists me to wear a shawl.

   More than a poem,
   It's a statement,
   The pain of a real women,
   Modesty in the name of culture, media.

   Sorry for all those…

❖ There are people out there
   whose lives are worse than ours,
   There are people out there
   whose lives are finer than ours,
   But no one has a life the same as ours

❖ Some people say,
   Don't try to understand everything
   That will mess up your mind,
   But it ain't like that.
   When you reach
   the point of understanding something
   completely
   you will start evolving

   Understanding is an endless process

❖ However, you are lost.
   The path cannot be found anywhere

❖ I never realized
I needed you.
I never realized
I needed people
Until I came out of the house.
And then, finally,
The days of illusion ended

❖ The love we have for each other
doesn't give me an opportunity
to give up on you, Mapla.
I won't

❖ Yeah, I must say
You meant the world to me
You mean the world to me
I saw the world through your screen
I learned from you
I enjoyed with you
I got angry with you
But I still love you
Future!?
I'm not sure about it
But I wish you'd stick with me
Dear Game

❖ The real Multiverse is Dreams

❖ Why, Am I selfish?
Or, am I stupid to love you only,
And not the people around you?
Oops, I forgot
Love differs from person to person

❖ The barrier of genders
Is already broken
When a child is born

Stop glorifying it

❖ Vazhkaiyehveh Spoiler la
Vazhra unaku
3 mani neram movie kuh
Spoiler paka mudila pathiya

❖ I hurt her
  After 90 days of pain
  Finally told her it's overwhelming
  She said, "Okay, be free"
  But I never told her
  Why I hurt her
  And here, finally after 4 years
  Just like we always used to talk
  Conveyed what happened actually

❖ Love
  Love
  Love, everywhere
  Everyone loves
  Everyone shares love
  But remember daughter and son
  The Humanity is the core

❖ I thought I'd be happy
   If I went away from home,
   Then suddenly realized
   place doesn't matter,
   It's the mind which is in trauma.
   But I realized one of the traumas
   Is not having people around
   When you're sick

❖ If you say, "No expectation in life",
   Then what about anger!?
   Anger is an emotion created
   when the expected thing
   doesn't happen, and
   When the unexpected thing happens

❖ ஆயிரம் கதைகள் சொல்லும்
   வாழ்க்கை
   நம் கதைகளை தவிர

❖ You broke the loop of months,
   Which made me happy.
   The time we had after that
   Was it friendship or gratitude?

❖ A year gonna pass
   Without watching the movies
   of the same year,
   I think

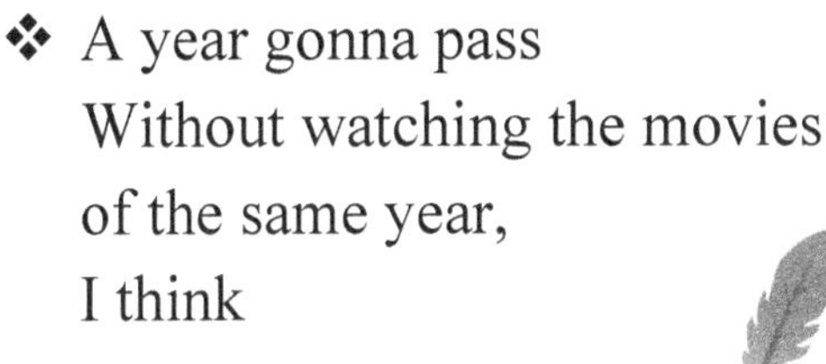

❖ There are people out there
   Who don't know me,
   I don't know them,
   But I still love them
   for their art

❖ : Why the peace can only be obtained
      after death!?
      Back off "Rip"
   : Hope you had a beautiful life out there

19

❖ : What are those eyes saying?
    What are those eyes trying to express?
    : Ney… ney… ney…
    I don't want to die
    I don't want to leave this world
    I don't want the drama to end
    Please save me

❖ : It was so confusing
    : What is so confusing?
    : The book
    The movie
    The Life
    : Ehhh
    It's okay, eventually
    You'll get a grab

❖ அறிமுகம் இல்லாத
சிறுவனின் தந்தை
"மாமா" என்று
அறிமுகம் செய்த்போது
எங்கிருந்தோ வந்தது
இனம்புரியா ஆனந்தம்

❖ : உனக்கு புடிச்ச மாதிரி இருந்துக்கோ
   : அத சொல்லனும்னு
     அவசியம் இல்ல

❖ I want to be by your side
   Beyond the end of time

❖ I was afraid of the end
   I didn't want to lose that
   'state of mind'
   So I used to watch just a bit per day
   Today, I felt it again

❖ I hope she will bring my softness
   Out of me

❖ When I see the people on stage,
   I like to say
   Let's play again

❖ Is that me?
Yes, Indeed

❖ The pain is same for all
Only we differ by perceiving

❖ One who caused the hurt is me
One who realized the mistake is me
One who asks for sorry is me
But one who got hurt is you,
Yet you chose to forgive.

I think,
I am starting to see
What it is like
To be forgiven by someone

❖ I feel like
you haven't given up on me
Like we used to be

- ❖ Sometimes I think
  If I could erase it…
  But then,
  No… It shouldn't be

- ❖ I feel so happy
  To have such a person in my life

- ❖ You are just deceiving me

- ❖ Maybe I have become
  Afraid of losing people too!

- ❖ Maybe I am just treating people
  the way she said
  'People are like passing clouds'
  But some crossed the clouds, though

- ❖ What am I gonna do without you!?

❖ I just lost the word
Which I wanted to say to you

❖ Yeah,
Conqueror is just a title for many
By influence, for us it's a dream
But I parted from my squad
in the process, I guess
When I finally achieved it
It made me happy, and
I just had memories of them
But in the process
I got a gem "Zig"

❖ I don't have much option
Other than moments and words
We got used

❖ I have never been so happy
For a show ending
Unfinished.
I even doubt that, I can say
These words for this show

❖ *நீ பன்னும்னு நெனச்ச விஷயத்த*
வேற யாரலையும்
நீ நெனச்ச மாதிரி பண்ணமுடியாது
So better *நீயே பன்னிடு*

❖ I'm crazy enough to say this
"When did I go away from you?"
- To dear cold

❖ The most typical thing in life is
People will change in a moment
or over time
By any kind of influence
But the problems begins
When the change meets society

❖ : Do I deserve this!?
: Maybe

❖ Unspoken words remind me
I'm still alive
But it also gives me frustration

❖ What if I die tomorrow!?
Will you cry!?
Will you smile!?
Will you mourn!?
Will you celebrate!?
Will you be happy!?
Will you be sad!?
Will you…
Maybe none of it matters after that or
Maybe it will be the utmost
important one

❖ இன்னொரு மனிதனை வெறுக்க
கற்றுத்தரும் அரசியல்
நமக்கு தேவையில்

Hope you all enjoyed the Poems, Thank you

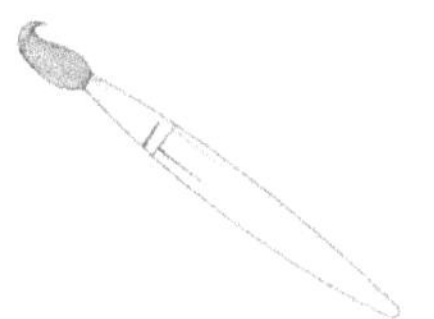

www.ingramcontent.com/pod-product-compliance
Lightning Source LLC
Chambersburg PA
CBHW040139150726
48005CB00015B/2563